Contents

About Science Centers
Grades 3–4

What's Great About This Book

Centers are a wonderful, fun way for students to practice important skills. The 14 centers in this book are self-contained and portable. Students may work at a desk, table, or even on the floor. Once you've made the centers, they're ready to use any time.

What's in This Book

Teacher direction page includes how to make the center and a description of the student task

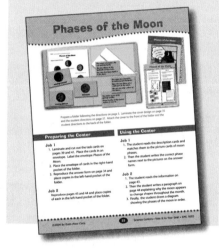

Full-color materials needed for the center

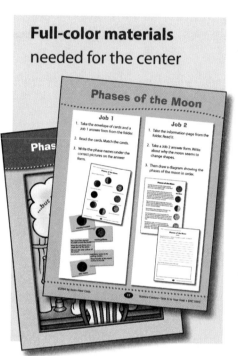

Reproducible answer forms

How to Use the Centers

The centers are intended for skill practice, not to introduce skills. It is important to model the use of each center before students do the task independently.

Questions to Consider:

- Will students select a center, or will you assign the centers?
- Will there be a specific block of time for centers, or will the centers be used throughout the day?
- Where will you place the centers for easy access by students?
- What procedure will students use when they need help with the center tasks?
- Where will students store completed work?
- How will you track the tasks and centers completed by each student?

Making a File Folder Center

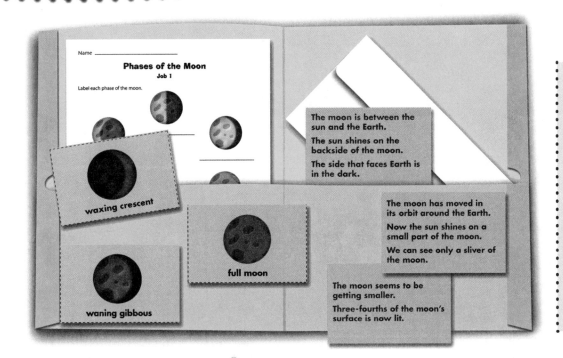

Materials

- folder with pockets
- envelopes
- marking pens
- glue
- tape

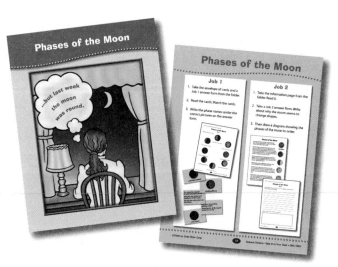

Steps to Follow

1. Laminate the cover design. Glue it to the front of the folder.

2. Laminate the student direction page. Glue it to the back of the folder.

3. Place answer forms, writing paper, and any other supplies in the left-hand pocket.

4. Place each set of task cards in an envelope. Place the envelope and sorting mat (if required for the center) in the right-hand pocket.

Center Checklist

Student Names

Centers

Centers											
Science Analogies											
Outer Space											
Phases of the Moon											
Vertebrate or Invertebrate?											
Mystery Animal											
Plant Parts											
Life Cycles											
Animal Adaptations											
Simple Machines											
Your Body Systems											
The Earth's Layers											
Sunlight to Night-light											
Solid, Liquid, or Gas?											
Food Webs											

Vertebrate or Invertebrate?

Prepare a folder following the directions on page 3. Laminate the cover design on page 47 and the student directions on page 49. Attach the cover to the front of the folder and the student directions to the back of the folder.

Preparing the Center

Job 1

1. Laminate the information pages on pages 51 and 53 and the picture cards on pages 55 and 57. Place the picture cards in an envelope. Label the envelope *Vertebrate or Invertebrate?*
2. Place the information pages and the envelope of picture cards in the right-hand pocket of the folder.
3. Reproduce the answer form on page 46 and place copies in the left-hand pocket of the folder.

Job 2

Reproduce pages 59 and 60 and place copies of each in the left-hand pocket of the folder.

Using the Center

Job 1

1. The student reads the definitions of vertebrates and invertebrates on the information pages.
2. The student divides the picture cards into two sets—vertebrates and invertebrates.
3. Then the student writes the animals' names under the correct heading on the answer form.

Job 2

1. The student takes only the vertebrate picture cards. The student reads the definitions on page 59. Then the student sorts the pictures into categories—birds, fish, mammals, reptiles, and amphibians.
2. The student writes the animals' names in the correct columns on the answer form.
3. Using page 60, the student draws an additional animal in each category.

Name _____

Vertebrate or Invertebrate?
Job 1

Vertebrates	Invertebrates
_____	_____
_____	_____
_____	_____
_____	_____
_____	_____
_____	_____
_____	_____
_____	_____
_____	_____
_____	_____
_____	_____
_____	_____

        Science Centers—Take It to Your Seat • EMC 5003

Vertebrate or Invertebrate?

A butterfly is an invertebrate.

It does **not** have a backbone.

A cat is a vertebrate.

It has a backbone.

Vertebrate or Invertebrate?

Job 1

1. Take the information pages, the envelope, and a Job 1 answer form from the folder.

2. Read the information pages.

3. Take the picture cards and sort them into vertebrates and invertebrates.

4. Write the animals' names in the correct columns on the answer form.

Job 2

1. Take the vertebrate picture cards and a Job 2—Part 1 and a Job 2—Part 2 answer form from the folder.

2. Read the information on the Job 2—Part 1 answer form. Sort the cards into categories.

3. Write the name of each animal in the correct place on the answer form.

4. Take the Job 2—Part 2 answer form and draw a new animal in each category.

Invertebrates

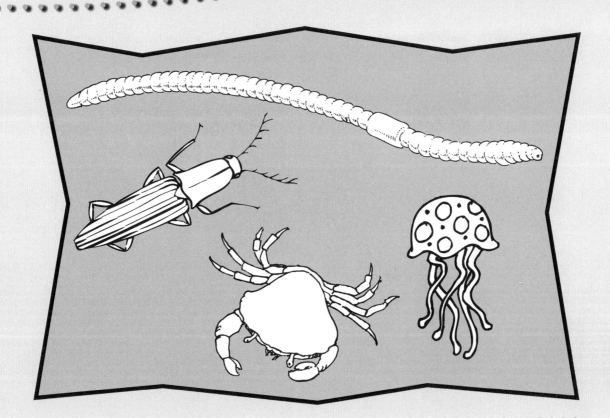

Invertebrates are animals that do not have an internal (inside) skeleton made of bone. They are sometimes called "animals without backbones."

Some invertebrates have a hard outer shell. Beetles and crabs are invertebrates with a hard outer shell. Some invertebrates have a soft outside. Worms and jellyfish are invertebrates with a soft outside.

There are many more invertebrates than vertebrates on Earth. Many are so small that we do not notice them in the same way we notice vertebrates.

Vertebrates

Vertebrates have an internal skeleton made of bone. They are sometimes called "animals with backbones."

There are many kinds of vertebrates. Some have feathers (birds). Some have scales (reptiles and fish). Others have hair (mammals). Some have skin with no scales, feathers, or hair (amphibians).

No matter what kind of outside covering they have, vertebrates have a skeleton of bone inside.

Science Centers—Take It to Your Seat • EMC 5003

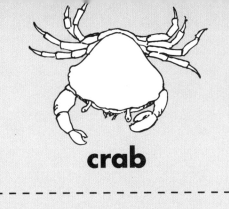

beetle

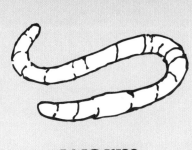

crab

worm

clam

snail

sea star

spider

dragonfly

grasshopper

scorpion

butterfly

octopus

bee

squid

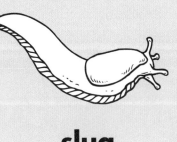

slug

goldfish

shark

tuna

frog

toad

**spotted
salamander**

snake

lizard

alligator

robin

parrot

chicken

gorilla

dog

horse

Name _____

Vertebrates
Job 2—Part 1

These animals are all kinds of vertebrates. They all have a backbone. Read about each kind. Look at the vertebrate cards. Write the name of each vertebrate on the correct line.

Mammal
A mammal has hair on some or most of its body.
A female mammal feeds milk from her body to her young.

1. _____   2. _____   3. _____

Fish
A fish is usually covered with scales.
Fish breathe with gills instead of lungs.

1. _____   2. _____   3. _____

Bird
A bird is covered with feathers.
It has wings, scaly legs, and a beak.
Female birds lay eggs.

1. _____   2. _____   3. _____

Reptile
A reptile is usually covered with dry scales or tough plates.
Reptiles slither across the ground or crawl on short legs.

1. _____   2. _____   3. _____

Amphibian
An amphibian has moist skin without scales, hair, or feathers.
It lives in water and breathes with gills when young.
It breathes with lungs as an adult.

1. _____   2. _____   3. _____

Name _____

Vertebrates
Job 2—Part 2

Draw one new animal in each category.
Then explain why the animal belongs in that category.

Bird	**Reptile**	**Mammal**

_____   _____   _____

_____   _____   _____

_____   _____   _____

Fish	**Amphibian**

_____   _____

_____   _____

_____   _____

Mystery Animal

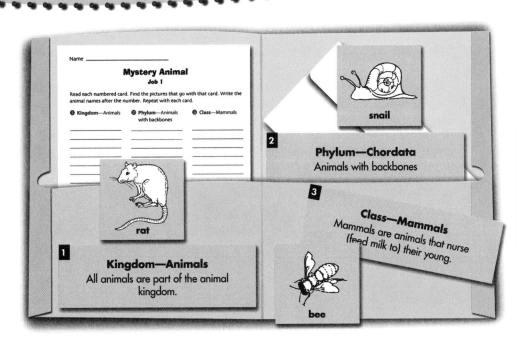

Prepare a folder following the directions on page 3. Laminate the cover design on page 63 and the student directions on page 65. Attach the cover to the front of the folder and the student directions to the back of the folder.

Preparing the Center

Job 1

1. Laminate and cut out pages 67, 69, and 71. Place the picture cards in an envelope labeled *Mystery Animal*.
2. Place the envelope and the numbered cards in the right-hand pocket of the folder.
3. Reproduce the answer form on page 62 and place copies in the left-hand pocket of the folder.

Job 2

Place a supply of drawing paper in the left-hand pocket of the folder.

Using the Center

Job 1

1. The student reads each numbered card one at a time and in order. After placing the card on the table, the student places the picture cards that fit that description in a row. Then the student writes the names of those living things on the answer form.
2. Next, the student reads card #2 and places it on top of card #1. The student removes the picture cards that no longer belong and writes the answers on the answer form.
3. The student repeats the steps with each numbered card until only one animal remains.

Job 2

1. The student takes a sheet of drawing paper and draws a favorite animal.
2. The student looks at the number cards, decides which fit the drawing, and writes the name and number of those descriptions on the drawing paper.

Name _____

Mystery Animal
Job 1

Read each numbered card. Find the pictures that go with that card. Write the animals' names below the number. Repeat with each card.

❶ Kingdom—Animals

_____
_____
_____
_____
_____
_____
_____
_____
_____

❷ Phylum—Animals with backbones

_____
_____
_____
_____
_____
_____
_____

❸ Class—Mammals

_____
_____
_____
_____
_____

❹ Order—Rodents

_____
_____
_____
_____

❺ Family—Rodents with bushy tails

_____
_____
_____

❻ Genus—Rodents with bushy tails that climb trees

_____
_____
_____

❼ Species—Rodents with bushy tails and gray fur that climb trees

The mystery animal is a _____.

Science Centers—Take It to Your Seat • EMC 5003

Mystery Animal

Mystery Animal

Job 1

1. Take an answer form and the envelope from the folder. Take Card 1 and read it.

2. Look at the picture cards. Choose the cards that fit the description. Place the cards in a row under Card 1.

3. Write the names of the pictures on the answer form.

4. Take Card 2. Read it and place it on top of Card 1. Look at the pictures and remove any that do <u>not</u> belong. Write the remaining names on the answer form.

5. Repeat the steps with each numbered card until only one animal remains.

Job 2

1. Take a sheet of writing paper from the folder. Draw your favorite animal.

2. Look at the numbered cards. Decide which descriptions fit your animal. Write the name and numbers on your paper.

1

Kingdom—Animals

All animals are part of the animal kingdom.

2

Phylum—Chordata

Animals with backbones

3

Class—Mammals

Mammals are animals that nurse (feed milk to) their young.

4

Order—Rodents

Rodents are mammals with long, sharp front teeth.

5

Family—Rodents with bushy tails

6

Genus—Rodents with bushy tails that climb trees

7

Species—Rodents with bushy tails and gray fur that climb trees

©2004 by Evan-Moor Corp.

©2004 by Evan-Moor Corp.

©2004 by Evan-Moor Corp.

tree

cactus

red squirrel

gray squirrel

chipmunk

beaver

rat

bear

bird

fish

snail

bee

Plant Parts

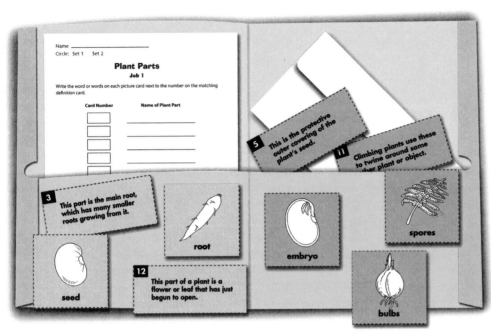

Prepare a folder following the directions on page 3. Laminate the cover design on page 75 and the student directions on page 77. Attach the cover to the front of the folder and the student directions to the back of the folder.

Preparing the Center

Job 1

1. Laminate and cut out the cards on pages 79, 81, 83, and 85. Place each set in an envelope. Label the envelopes *Plant Parts— Set 1* and *Plant Parts—Set 2*.

2. Place the envelopes in the right-hand pocket of the folder.

3. Reproduce the answer form on page 74 and place copies in the left-hand pocket of the folder.

Job 2

Reproduce pages 87 and 88 and place copies of each in the left-hand pocket of the folder.

Using the Center

Job 1

1. The student takes an envelope and circles the set number on the answer form.

2. The student reads the definition cards and matches them with the correct picture cards.

3. Then the student writes the name of the picture next to its definition number on the answer form.

Job 2

1. The student labels the parts of a plant on page 87.

2. Then the student completes the crossword puzzle on page 88.

Name _____

Circle: Set 1   Set 2

Plant Parts

Job 1

Write the word or words on each picture card next to the number on the matching definition card.

Card Number	Name of Plant Part
	_____
	_____
	_____
	_____
	_____
	_____
	_____
	_____
	_____
	_____
	_____

Plant Parts

Plant Parts

Job 1

1. Take a Job 1 answer form and one envelope from the folder. Circle the set number.

2. Read each numbered card. Match it to the correct picture card.

3. Write the word or words on the picture card next to the number on the answer form.

Job 2

1. Take a Job 2—Part 1 answer form from the folder. Label the parts of the plant.

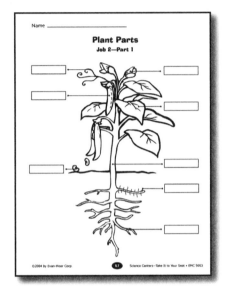

2. Take a Job 2—Part 2 answer form. Do the crossword puzzle.

1 This part of a plant holds it upright in the soil. It collects water and nutrients from the soil and carries them to the stem. It stores foods.

2 These are thin roots that spread out in all directions just below the surface of the soil.

3 This part is the main root, which has many smaller roots growing from it.

4 This is the part of a plant that absorbs sunlight and makes food for the plant.

5 This part holds the plant upright. It carries water and nutrients from the roots to the leaves.

6 This part of the plant is where seeds are produced. It is colorful. It may produce sweet nectar or sweet smelling perfume.

7 These are the colorful parts of a flower.

8 This is the part of a flowering plant that grows into a new plant.

9 This part of a plant develops from a flower. It contains one or more seeds. Sometimes it can be eaten.

10 These are the stems growing off the main stem or trunk of a tree, bush, or shrub.

11 This is the main stem of a tree.

12 This part of a plant is a flower or leaf that has just begun to open.

Set 1

Set 1

Set 1

Set 1

Set 1

Set 1

Set 1

Set 1

Set 1

Set 1

Set 1

Set 1

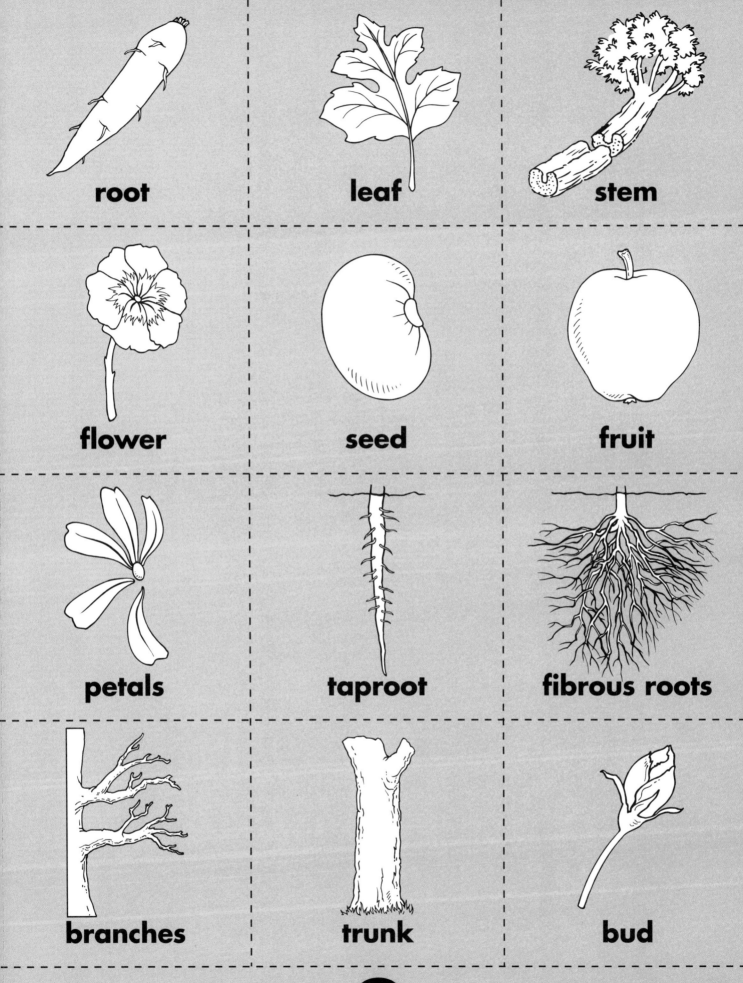

root

leaf

stem

flower

seed

fruit

petals

taproot

fibrous roots

branches

trunk

bud

Set 1

Set 1

Set 1

Set 1

Set 1

Set 1

Set 1

Set 1

Set 1

Set 1

Set 1

Set 1

1 These are the tiny parts of a root that absorb water from the ground.

2 This part of the plant protects the root tip as it grows and pushes through the soil.

3 This is what it is called when a plant loses water through its leaves.

4 This is the growing part of a plant's seed.

5 This is the protective outer covering of the plant's seed.

6 Plants such as tulips do not grow from seeds. They grow from this plant part.

7 Nonflowering plants such as ferns do not produce seeds. New plants grow from these.

8 This occurs when pollen from one flower's stamen reaches another flower's stigma. Wind, insects, and birds help move the pollen.

9 This is what it is called when a plant makes food in its leaves.

10 Some plants use these for protection.

11 Climbing plants use these to twine around some other plant or object.

12 This is the green part of a plant that collects the sun's energy to make its food.

Set 2

Set 2

Set 2

Set 2

Set 2

Set 2

Set 2

Set 2

Set 2

Set 2

Set 2

Set 2

 **root hairs**

 **root cap**

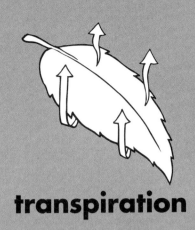 **transpiration**

 **embryo**

seed coat

 **bulb**

 **spores**

 **pollination**

 **photosynthesis**

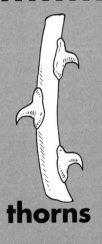 **thorns**

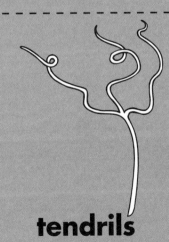 **tendrils**

 **chlorophyll**

Set 2

Set 2

Set 2

Set 2

Set 2

Set 2

Set 2

Set 2

Set 2

Set 2

Set 2

Set 2

Name _____

Plant Parts

Job 2—Part 1

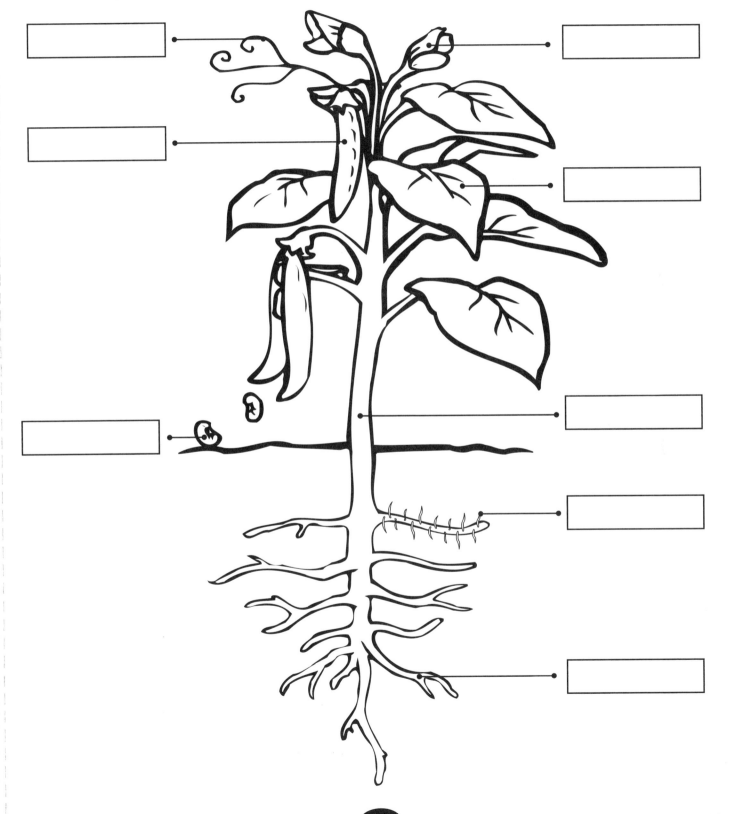

87

Name _____

Plant Parts
Job 2—Part 2

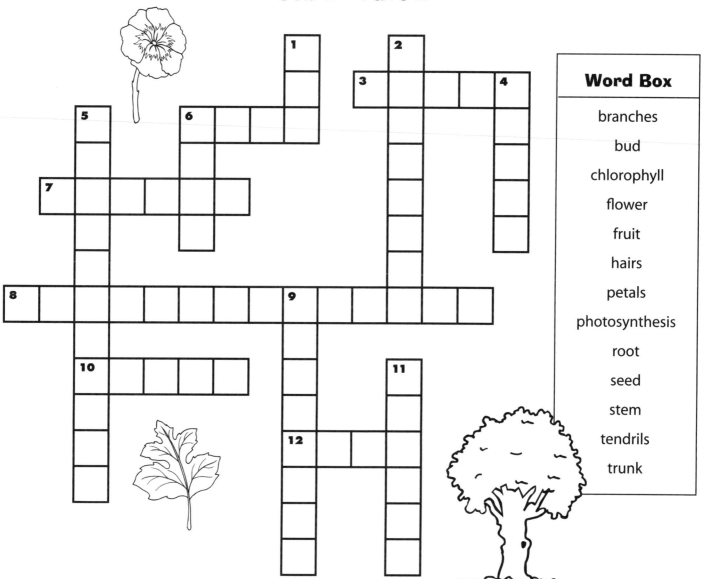

Word Box

branches
bud
chlorophyll
flower
fruit
hairs
petals
photosynthesis
root
seed
stem
tendrils
trunk

Across

3. the part that contains the seeds
6. the part that grows into a new plant
7. the part where seeds are produced
8. _____ is when a plant makes food in its leaves
10. the tiny parts of a root that absorb water from the ground are called root _____
12. the part of a plant that draws nourishment from the soil and stores food

Down

1. a leaf or flower that has just begun to open
2. stems growing off the main trunk of a tree
4. the main stem of a tree
5. the green part of a leaf that helps make food for the plant
6. the part that holds the plant upright
9. the parts used by climbing plants to twine around other objects
11. the colorful part of a flower

Life Cycles

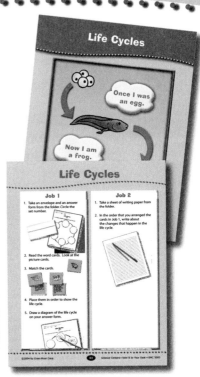

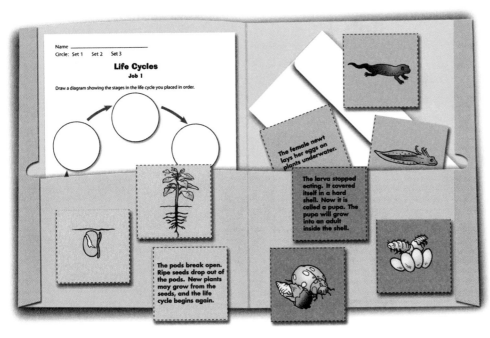

Prepare a folder following the directions on page 3. Laminate the cover design on page 91 and the student directions on page 93. Attach the cover to the front of the folder and the student directions to the back of the folder.

Preparing the Center

Job 1

1. Laminate and cut out the cards on pages 95, 97, and 99. Place each set in an envelope labeled *Bean—Set 1, Ladybird Beetle—Set 2,* and *Newt—Set 3.*
2. Place the envelopes in the right-hand pocket of the folder.
3. Reproduce the answer form on page 90 and place copies in the left-hand pocket of the folder.

Job 2

Place a supply of writing paper in the left-hand pocket of the folder.

Using the Center

Job 1

1. The student selects one envelope and circles the set number on the answer form.
2. The student reads the information on each card, matches it to the correct picture card, and then arranges the cards in order from the seed or egg to the adult form.
3. Finally, the student draws a diagram of the life cycle on the answer form.

Job 2

The student writes a description of the changes that occur in the life cycle sequenced in Job 1.

Name _____

Circle: Set 1   Set 2   Set 3

Life Cycles
Job 1

Draw a diagram showing the stages in the life cycle you placed in order.

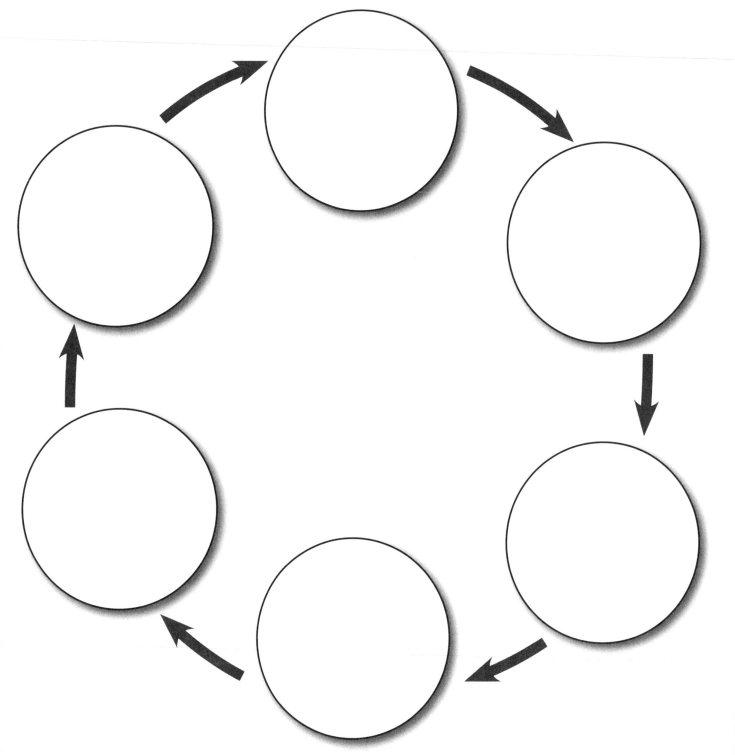

Life Cycles

Science Centers—Take It to Your Seat • EMC 5003

Life Cycles

Job 1

1. Take an envelope and an answer form from the folder. Circle the set number.

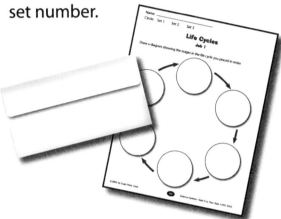

2. Read the word cards. Look at the picture cards.

3. Match the cards.

4. Place them in order to show the life cycle.

5. Draw a diagram of the life cycle on your answer form.

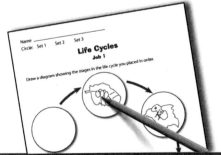

Job 2

1. Take a sheet of writing paper from the folder.

2. In the order that you arranged the cards in Job 1, write about the changes that happen in the life cycle.

Science Centers—Take It to Your Seat • EMC 5003

Science Centers—Take It to Your Seat • EMC 5003

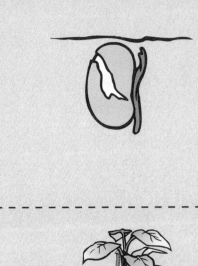 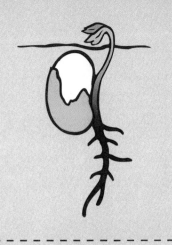 

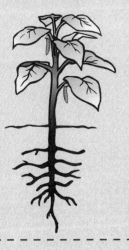  

When a seed starts to grow (germinate), the roots and a stem break through the seed coat.

The plant is growing. It has a few leaves. The seedling uses food stored in the seed to grow the leaves.

The plant is growing bigger. It has more leaves. The leaves use sunlight and water to make food for the plant.

Seeds are growing inside the pods on the bean plant.

The pods break open. Ripe seeds drop out of the pods. New plants may grow from the seeds, and the life cycle begins again.

The plant is grown now. It has flowers. The flowers will make seeds.

Set 1

Set 1

Set 1

Set 1

Set 1

Set 1

Set 1

Set 1

Set 1

Set 1

Set 1

Set 1

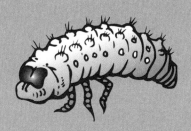

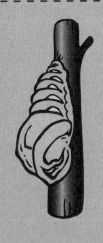

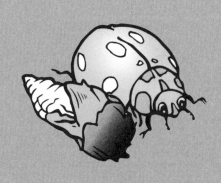

The female ladybird beetle lays her eggs on a leaf.

It has been about one week. The larvae hatch from the eggs. They don't look like ladybird beetles yet.

The larva eats and eats. It grows quickly. It sheds its skin (molts) several times as it grows.

The larva stops eating. It covers itself in a hard shell. Now it is called a pupa. The pupa will grow into an adult inside the shell.

When an adult ladybird beetle breaks out of its shell, it is yellow. In a short time, it will turn red.

The ladybird beetle is an adult now. The female will soon be ready to lay eggs. The life cycle will begin again.

Set 2

Set 2

Set 2

Set 2

Set 2

Set 2

Set 2

Set 2

Set 2

Set 2

Set 2

Set 2

  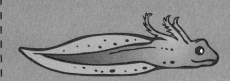

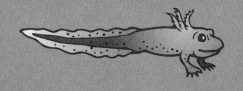  

The female newt lays her eggs on plants underwater.

A newt larva hatches from an egg.

The newt larva has feathery gills for breathing underwater.

The newt grows its front legs first.

The newt grows its back legs. Lungs have replaced its gills. It must go to the surface of the water to breathe air.

The adult newt leaves the water where it hatched. It returns to the water to wet its skin. The female returns when it is time to lay her eggs. The cycle will begin again.

Set 3

Set 3

Set 3

Set 3

Set 3

Set 3

Set 3

Set 3

Set 3

Set 3

Set 3

Set 3

Animal Adaptations

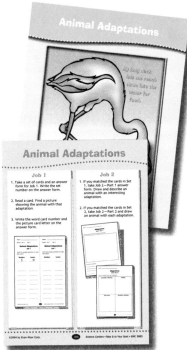

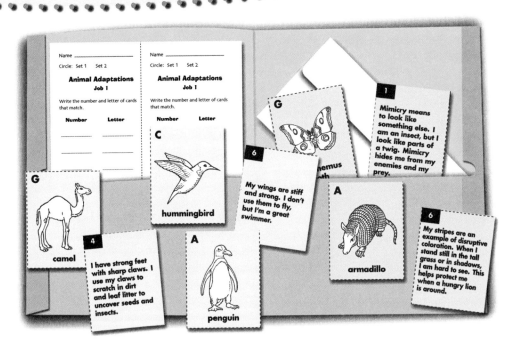

Prepare a folder following the directions on page 3. Laminate the cover design on page 103 and the student directions on page 105. Attach the cover to the front of the folder and the student directions to the back of the folder.

Preparing the Center

Job 1

1. Laminate and cut out the cards on pages 107 through 113. Place each set of cards in an envelope labeled *Animal Adaptations—Set 1* and *Animal Adaptations—Set 2*.
2. Place both envelopes in the right-hand pocket of the folder.
3. Reproduce the answer forms on page 102 and place copies in the left-hand pocket of the folder.

Job 2

Reproduce pages 115 and 116 and place copies of each in the left-hand pocket of the folder.

Using the Center

Job 1

1. The student selects an envelope of cards, circles the set number on the answer form, reads the description of an adaptation, and then selects the picture card showing an animal with that adaptation.
2. Then the student writes the letter and number of the cards that match on the answer form.

Job 2

1. If the student matched the cards in Set 1, he or she takes page 115 and draws and describes an animal with an interesting adaptation.
2. If the student matched the cards in Set 2, he or she takes page 116 and draws an animal with each adaptation.

Circle: Set 1   Set 2

Animal Adaptations
Job 1

Write the number and letter of the cards that match.

Number	Letter
_____	_____
_____	_____
_____	_____
_____	_____
_____	_____
_____	_____
_____	_____
_____	_____

Name _____

Circle: Set 1   Set 2

Animal Adaptations
Job 1

Write the number and letter of the cards that match.

Number	Letter
_____	_____
_____	_____
_____	_____
_____	_____
_____	_____
_____	_____
_____	_____
_____	_____

Animal Adaptations

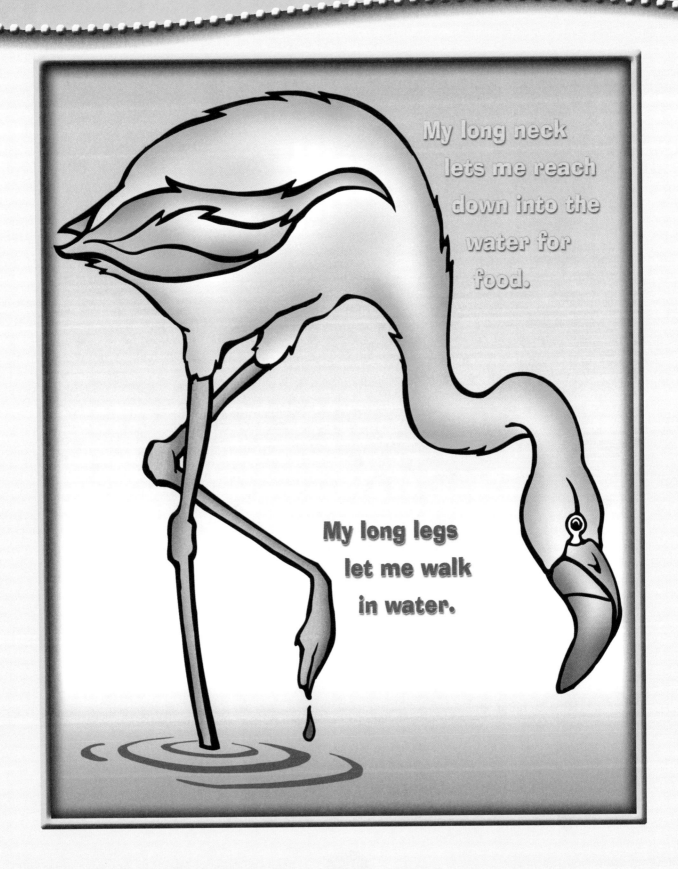

Animal Adaptations

Job 1

1. Take an envelope and a Job 1 answer form from the folder. Circle the set number.

2. Read a card. Find a picture showing the animal with that adaptation.

3. Write the word card number and the picture card letter on the answer form.

Job 2

1. If you matched the cards in Set 1, take a Job 2—Part 1 answer form from the folder. Draw and describe an animal with an interesting adaptation.

2. If you matched the cards in Set 2, take a Job 2—Part 2 answer form and draw an animal with each adaptation.

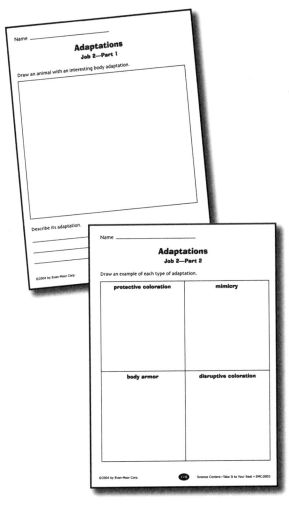

Science Centers—Take It to Your Seat • EMC 5003

1

I have a long bill that works like a straw so I can sip nectar from flowers.

2

My sharp hooked beak is used to catch and kill live prey. I use it to tear off pieces small enough to swallow.

3

My webbed feet can paddle through the water and walk on mud.

4

I have strong feet with sharp claws. I use my claws to scratch in dirt and leaf litter to uncover seeds and insects.

5

My long legs make it possible for me to eat the leaves off tree branches. My long neck can bend down so I can drink water and eat plants low to the ground.

6

My wings are stiff and strong. I don't use them to fly, but I'm a great swimmer.

7

My long arms may look strange, but I can reach a long way for food in trees. My arms are great for swinging from branch to branch, too.

8

My ears are so big they look like they should belong to a larger animal. They are perfect for a desert animal like me. My big ears let heat escape and keep my body cool.

9

My long eyelashes protect my eyes from blowing sand. I can close my nostrils to keep out blowing sand, too.

Set 1

Set 1

Set 1

Set 1

Set 1

Set 1

Set 1

Set 1

Set 1

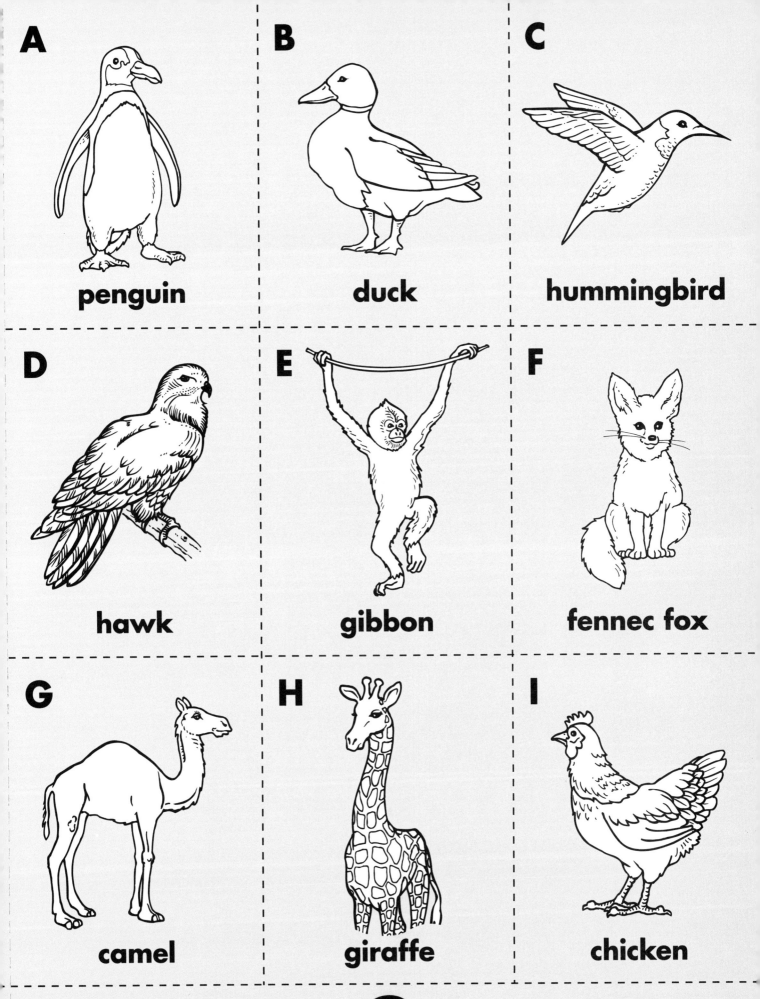

A penguin

B duck

C hummingbird

D hawk

E gibbon

F fennec fox

G camel

H giraffe

I chicken

Set 1

Set 1

Set 1

Set 1

Set 1

Set 1

Set 1

Set 1

Set 1

1

Mimicry means to look like something else. I am an insect, but I look like parts of a twig. Mimicry hides me from my enemies and my prey.

2

Mimicry means to look like something else. I use mimicry to hide from my enemies. Although I am an insect, I look like a leaf on a plant.

3

The markings on my wings look like the eyes of a large animal. My eyespots startle hungry birds away.

4

It can be dangerous for a small animal in my underwater habitat. I use protective coloration to hide from danger. I quickly change the color and pattern of my skin when an enemy is near.

5

I use protective coloration to hide from my enemies. My fur is brown most of the year, but it turns white when winter comes. I can hide in the snow. Only my black nose can give me away.

6

My stripes are an example of disruptive coloration. When I stand still in the tall grass or in shadows, I am hard to see. This helps protect me when a hungry lion is around.

7

I am small, but I have a mighty adaptation. I can spray my enemies with a liquid that smells horrible. If you get my spray on your body or in your eyes, you will leave me alone.

8

I am one of the animals that has body armor for protection. If danger comes too close, I roll up into a ball so my thick scales protect me from harm.

9

I may be small, but I'm not harmless. My bright color warns other animals that I am poisonous. It's best to leave me alone!

Set 2

Set 2

Set 2

Set 2

Set 2

Set 2

Set 2

Set 2

Set 2

A
armadillo

B
skunk

C
katydid

D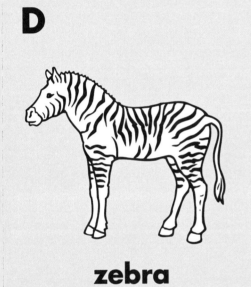
zebra

E
poison dart frog

F
arctic fox

G
**polyphemus
moth**

H
cuttlefish

I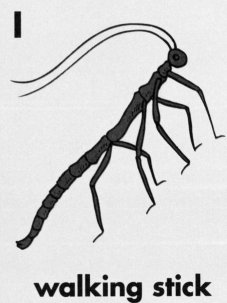
walking stick

Set 2

Set 2

Set 2

Set 2

Set 2

Set 2

Set 2

Set 2

Set 2

Name _____

Animal Adaptations
Job 2—Part 1

Draw an animal with an interesting body adaptation.

Describe its adaptation.

_____

_____

_____

Name _____

Animal Adaptations
Job 2—Part 2

Draw an example of each type of adaptation.

protective coloration	mimicry
body armor	**disruptive coloration**

Science Centers—Take It to Your Seat • EMC 5003

Simple Machines

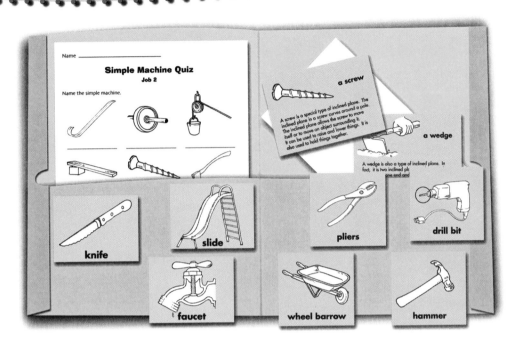

Prepare a folder following the directions on page 3. Laminate the cover design on page 119 and the student directions on page 121. Attach the cover to the front of the folder and the student directions to the back of the folder.

Preparing the Center

Job 1

1. Laminate and cut out the information cards on page 123 and the picture cards on pages 125 and 127. Place the picture cards in an envelope labeled *Simple Machines*.
2. Place the information cards and the envelope in the right-hand pocket of the folder.
3. Reproduce the answer form on page 118 and place copies in the left-hand pocket of the folder.

Job 2

Reproduce pages 129 and 130 and place copies of each in the left-hand pocket of the folder.

Using the Center

Job 1

1. The student reads the information cards.
2. Then the student removes the picture cards from the envelope. After placing the information cards in a row, the student decides what kind of simple machine each tool represents and places it under the correct description.
3. Finally, the student lists the tools in each category on the answer form.

Job 2

1. The student completes the Simple Machines Quiz on page 129.
2. Then if the student is ready for a challenge, he or she completes the Simple Machines Challenge on page 130.

Name _____

Simple Machines
Job 1

Write the tool names in the correct boxes.

inclined plane	wedge	lever
_____	_____	_____
_____	_____	_____
_____	_____	_____
_____	_____	_____
screw	**pulley**	**wheel and axle**
_____	_____	_____
_____	_____	_____
_____	_____	_____
_____	_____	_____

Simple Machines

Simple Machines

Job 1

1. Take a Job 1 answer form, the information cards, and the envelope from the folder.

2. Read the information cards.

3. Place the information cards in a row.

4. Look at the picture cards. Decide what goes in each group and place it under the correct description.

5. List the correct tools in each box on the answer form.

Job 2

1. Take a Job 2—Part 1 answer form from the folder. Answer the questions on the Simple Machines Quiz.

2. If you like a challenge, take a Job 2—Part 2 answer form and complete the Simple Machines Challenge.

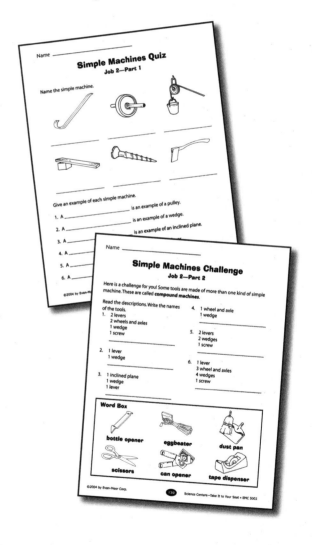

122

Simple Machines

A simple machine is a machine with few or no moving parts. Simple machines make our work easier.

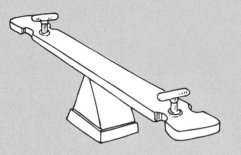

a lever

A lever is a bar that moves on a turning point. The bar can be straight or curved. This simple machine helps us move things by pushing, pulling, or lifting. You could use a lever to pry a nail out of a board.

a wheel and axle

A wheel and axle moves objects across a distance. This simple machine is a wheel (round part) that turns the axle. The axle (a smaller cylinder) is fastened to the wheel so they turn together.

a pulley

This simple machine uses wheels and a rope to move objects up, down, and across a long distance. Instead of an axle, the wheel is used to turn a rope or cord. The cord wraps around a wheel. As the wheel turns, the cord moves. Attach a hook to the cord and you can raise and lower objects.

an inclined plane

A plane is a flat surface. If one end of the plane surface is raised higher than the other, you have a simple machine called an inclined plane. It makes the work of moving things up and down easier.

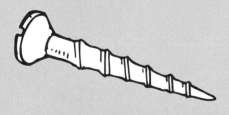

a screw

A screw is a special type of inclined plane. The inclined plane in a screw curves around a pole. The inclined plane allows the screw to move itself or to move an object surrounding it. It can be used to raise and lower things. It is also used to hold things together.

a wedge

A wedge is also a type of inclined plane. In fact, it is two inclined planes working together. It is wide at one end and tapers to a point at the other end. It is used to separate things by cutting, piercing, or splitting.

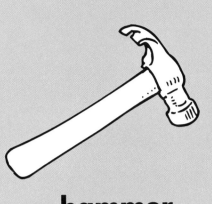

hammer

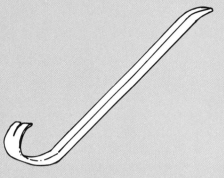

crowbar

pliers

bottle opener

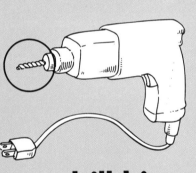

wheel barrow

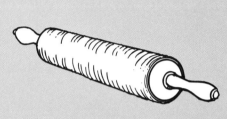

rolling pin

toy car

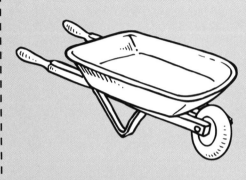

drill bit

flagpole

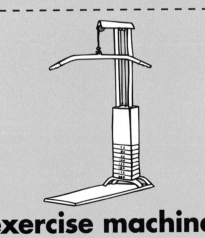

exercise machine

crane

miniblinds

slide

ramp

escalator

stairs

bicycle

corkscrew

bolt

faucet

teeth

knife

saw

needle

Name _____

Simple Machines Quiz
Job 2—Part 1

Name the simple machine.

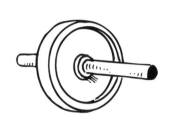

_____   _____   _____

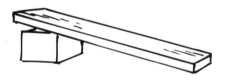

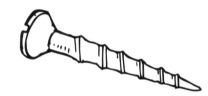

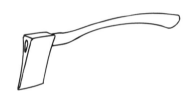

_____   _____   _____

Give an example of each simple machine.

1. A _____ is an example of a pulley.

2. A _____ is an example of a wedge.

3. A _____ is an example of an inclined plane.

4. A _____ is an example of a lever.

5. A _____ is an example of a wheel and axle.

6. A _____ is an example of a screw.

Name _____

Simple Machines Challenge
Job 2—Part 2

Here is a challenge for you! Some tools are made of more than one kind of simple machine. These are called **compound machines**.

Read the descriptions. Write the names of the tools.

1. 2 levers
    2 wheels and axles
    1 wedge
    1 screw

    _____

2. 1 lever
    1 wedge

    _____

3. 1 inclined plane
    1 wedge
    1 lever

    _____

4. 1 wheel and axle
    1 wedge

    _____

5. 2 levers
    2 wedges
    1 screw

    _____

6. 1 lever
    3 wheel and axles
    4 wedges
    1 screw

    _____

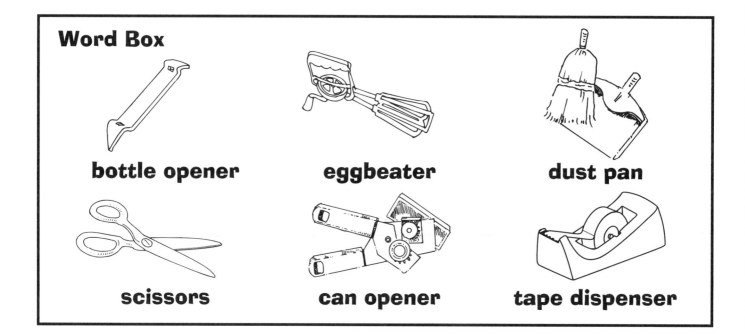

Word Box

bottle opener   eggbeater   dust pan

scissors   can opener   tape dispenser

                   Science Centers—Take It to Your Seat • EMC 5003

Your Body Systems

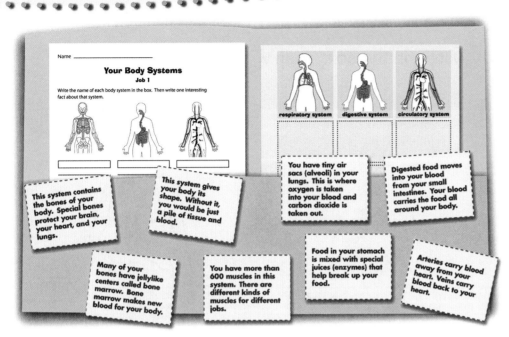

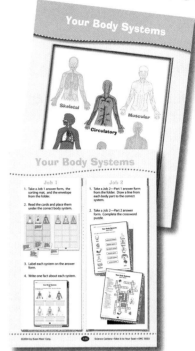

Prepare a folder following the directions on page 3. Laminate the cover design on page 133 and the student directions on page 135. Attach the cover to the front of the folder and the student directions to the back of the folder.

Preparing the Center

Job 1

1. Tape the sorting mat on pages 137 and 139 together. Laminate it and fold in half before placing it in the right-hand pocket of the folder.
2. Laminate and cut out the cards on pages 141 and 143. Place the cards in an envelope labeled *Your Body Systems* and place it in the right-hand pocket of the folder.
3. Reproduce the answer form on page 132 and place copies in the left-hand pocket of the folder.

Job 2

Reproduce pages 145 and 146 and place copies of each in the left-hand pocket of the folder.

Using the Center

Job 1

1. The student reads the cards, placing each one on the sorting mat below the correct body system illustration.
2. Then the student labels each system on the answer form and writes one fact about it.

Job 2

1. On page 145, the student draws a line to match a body part to the correct system.
2. On page 146, the student completes a crossword puzzle about body parts.

Name _____

Your Body Systems
Job 1

Write the name of each body system in the box. Then write one interesting
fact about that system.

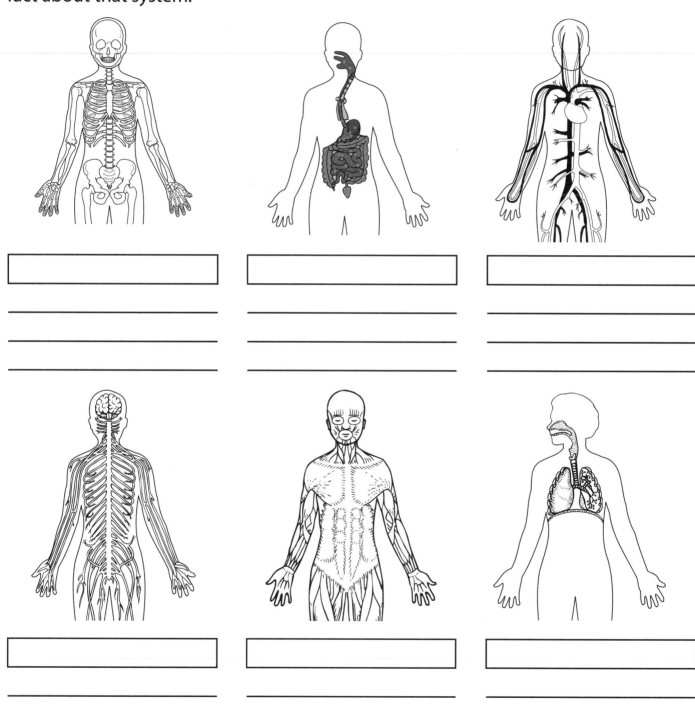

Your Body Systems

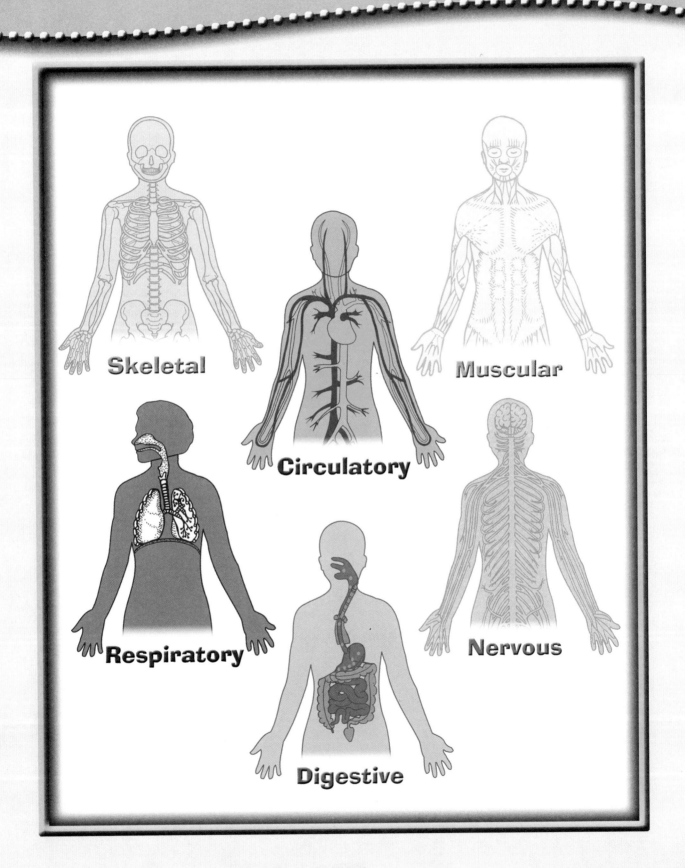

Skeletal

Circulatory

Muscular

Respiratory

Digestive

Nervous

Your Body Systems

Job 1

1. Take a Job 1 answer form, the sorting mat, and the envelope from the folder.

2. Read the cards and place them under the correct body system.

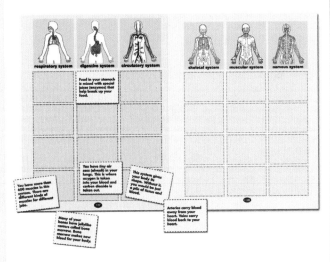

3. Label each system on the answer form.

4. Write one fact about each system.

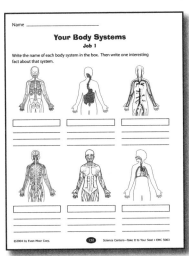

Job 2

1. Take a Job 2—Part 1 answer form from the folder. Draw a line from each body part to the correct system.

2. Take a Job 2—Part 2 answer form. Complete the crossword puzzle.

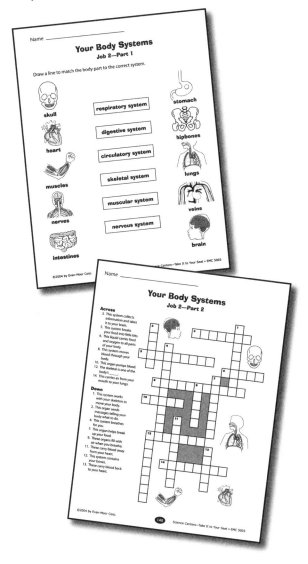

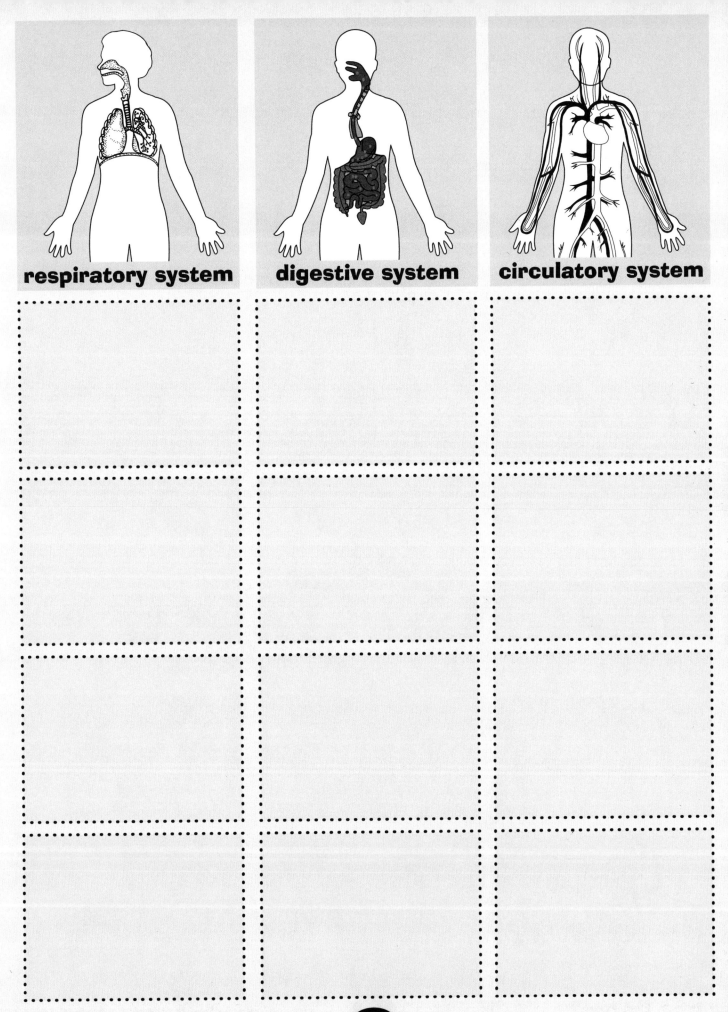

respiratory system

digestive system

circulatory system

Science Centers—Take It to Your Seat • EMC 5003

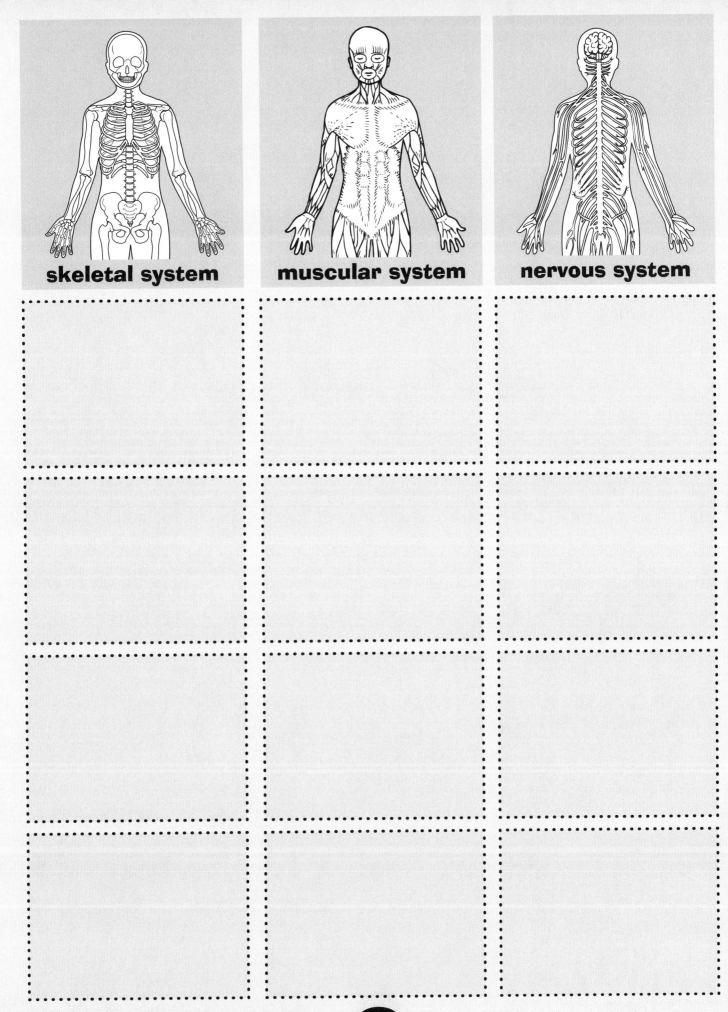

skeletal system

muscular system

nervous system

This system is the part of the body that breathes for you.

You have tiny air sacs (alveoli) in your lungs. This is where oxygen is taken into your blood and carbon dioxide is taken out.

This system contains your lungs.

Your windpipe (trachea) carries air from your mouth to your lungs.

This system is like a food blender. It breaks your food into little bits.

Food in your stomach is mixed with special juices (enzymes) that help break up your food.

Digested food moves into your blood from your small intestines. Your blood carries the food all around your body.

This system gets rid of the food you cannot digest. It is packed together and leaves your body when you go to the bathroom.

This system contains your heart, the muscle that pumps your blood.

Blood carries digested food to all parts of your body. It carries oxygen to all parts of your body.

Arteries carry blood away from your heart. Veins carry blood back to your heart.

White blood cells in your blood attack and eat germs.

This system contains the bones of your body. Special bones protect your brain, your heart, and your lungs.

This system gives your body its shape. Without it, you would be just a pile of tissue and blood.

This system works with your muscles to move your body.

Many of your bones have jellylike centers called bone marrow. Bone marrow makes new blood for your body.

This system works with your skeleton to move your body.

You have more than 600 muscles in this system. There are different kinds of muscles for different jobs.

Muscles can pull, but they cannot push.

Strong bands (tendons) hold your muscles to your bones.

This system receives information collected by your five senses (sight, hearing, smell, taste, touch).

This system contains your brain. Your brain sends messages to all parts of your body, telling it what to do.

Nerves run throughout your body. Electrical signals carry information along nerves to your brain.

You don't have to think about making your heart beat or your lungs breathe. A special part of this system makes that happen.

Name _____

Your Body Systems
Job 2—Part 1

Draw a line to match the body part to the correct system.

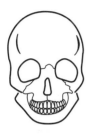

skull

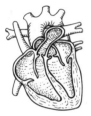

heart

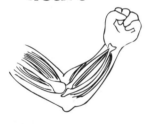

muscles

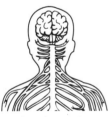

nerves

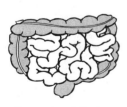

intestines

| respiratory system |

| digestive system |

| circulatory system |

| skeletal system |

| muscular system |

| nervous system |

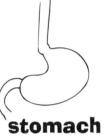

stomach

hipbones

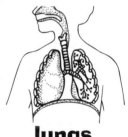

lungs

veins

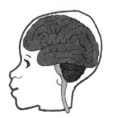

brain

Science Centers—Take It to Your Seat • EMC 5003

Your Body Systems
Job 2—Part 2

Across

3. This system collects information and takes it to your brain.
5. This system breaks your food into little bits.
6. This liquid carries food and oxygen to all parts of your body.
8. This system moves blood through your body.
10. This organ pumps blood.
12. The skeletal is one of the body's _____.
14. This carries air from your mouth to your lungs.

Down

1. This system works with your skeleton to move your body.
2. This organ sends messages telling your body what to do.
4. This system breathes for you.
7. This organ helps break up your food.
9. These organs fill with air when you breathe.
11. These carry blood away from your heart.
12. This system contains your bones.
13. These carry blood back to your heart.

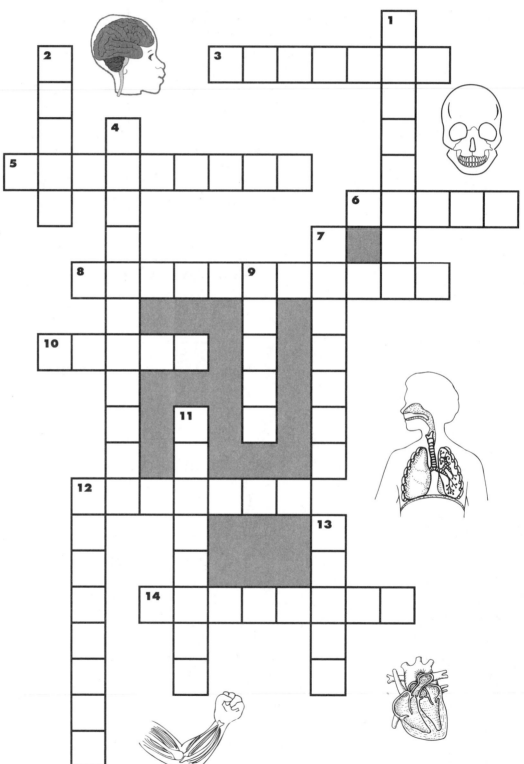

Science Centers—Take It to Your Seat • EMC 5003

The Earth's Layers

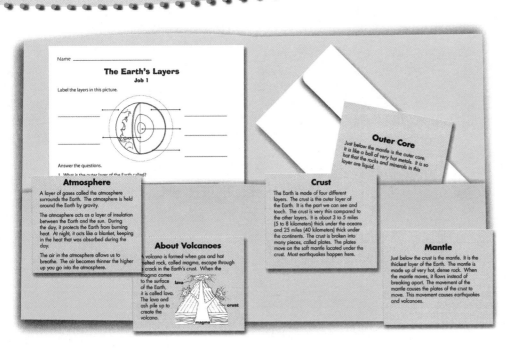

Prepare a folder following the directions on page 3. Laminate the cover design on page 149 and the student directions on page 151. Attach the cover to the front of the folder and the student directions to the back of the folder.

Preparing the Center

Job 1

1. Laminate and cut out the information cards on page 153. Place the five layer cards in an envelope labeled *The Earth's Layers*. Place the volcano card in an envelope labeled *About Volcanoes*.
2. Place both envelopes in the right-hand pocket of the folder.
3. Reproduce the answer form on page 148 and place copies in the left-hand pocket of the folder.

Job 2

Provide a supply of writing paper in the left-hand pocket of the folder.

Using the Center

Job 1

1. The student takes the envelope of cards labeled *The Earth's Layers* and the answer form.
2. After reading each card, the student labels that layer on the diagram on the answer form.
3. Using the information from the cards, the student answers the questions on the answer form.

Job 2

1. The student takes a sheet of paper and the envelope containing the volcano card.
2. After reading the card, the student draws a volcano erupting.
3. Then the student writes a brief description of what happens during an eruption.

Name _____

The Earth's Layers
Job 1

Label the layers in this picture.

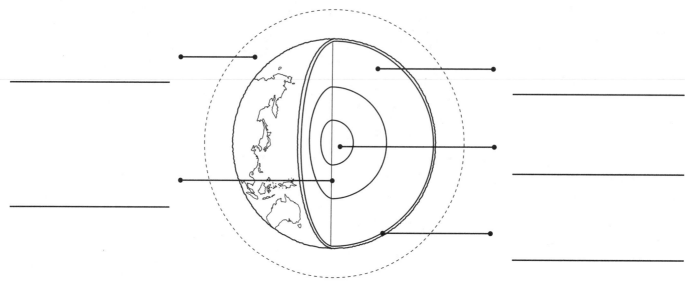

Answer the questions.

1. What is the outer layer of the Earth called?

_____

2. What is the mantle made of?

_____

3. What is the layer of air surrounding the Earth called?

_____

4. Which layer of the Earth is the thickest?

_____

5. What keeps the metals at the center of the Earth from moving?

_____

6. List two ways the atmosphere helps the Earth.

_____

7. Is the Earth's crust thicker under the oceans or under the continents?

_____

8. What causes volcanoes to form?

_____

The Earth's Layers

150

The Earth's Layers

Job 1

1. Take the envelope of cards labeled *The Earth's Layers* and an answer form from the folder.

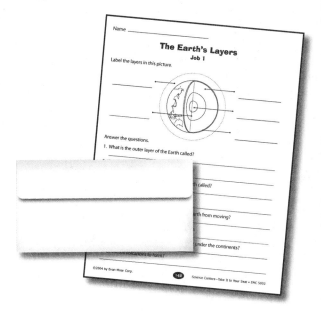

2. Read each card and label the layer that it describes.

3. Answer the questions.

Job 2

1. Take a sheet of paper and the envelope containing the volcano card from the folder.

2. Read the card. Then draw a volcano erupting.

3. Write a description of what is happening.

Science Centers—Take It to Your Seat • EMC 5003

Atmosphere

A layer of gases called the atmosphere surrounds the Earth. The atmosphere is held around the Earth by gravity.

The atmosphere acts as a layer of insulation between the Earth and the sun. During the day, it protects the Earth from burning heat. At night, it acts like a blanket, keeping in the heat that was absorbed during the day.

The air in the atmosphere allows us to breathe. The air becomes thinner the higher up you go into the atmosphere.

Crust

The Earth is made of four different layers. The crust is the outer layer of the Earth. It is the part we can see and touch. The crust is very thin compared to the other layers. It is about 3 to 5 miles (5 to 8 kilometers) thick under the oceans and 25 miles (40 kilometers) thick under the continents. The crust is broken into many pieces, called plates. The plates move on the soft mantle located under the crust. Most earthquakes happen here.

Mantle

Just below the crust is the mantle. It is the thickest layer of the Earth. The mantle is made up of very hot, dense rock. When the mantle moves, it flows instead of breaking apart. The movement of the mantle causes the plates of the crust to move. This movement causes earthquakes and volcanoes.

Outer Core

Just below the mantle is the outer core. It is like a ball of very hot metals. It is so hot that the rocks and minerals in this layer are liquid.

Inner Core

Below the outer core at the center of the Earth is the inner core. The temperature and pressure are so great that the metals are squeezed together and are not able to move.

About Volcanoes

A volcano is formed when gas and hot melted rock, called magma, escape through a crack in the Earth's crust. When the magma comes to the surface of the Earth, it is called lava. The lava and ash pile up to create the volcano.

lava

crust

magma

Sunlight to Night-light

Prepare a folder following the directions on page 3. Laminate the cover design on page 157 and the student directions on page 159. Attach the cover to the front of the folder and the student directions to the back of the folder.

Preparing the Center

Job 1

1. Laminate and cut out the cards on pages 161 through 164. Place the cards in an envelope labeled *Sunlight to Night-light*.
2. Place the envelope in the right-hand pocket of the folder.
3. Reproduce the answer form on page 156 and place copies in the left-hand pocket of the folder.

Job 2

Reproduce pages 165 and 166 and place copies of each in the left-hand pocket of the folder.

Using the Center

Job 1

1. The student takes the picture cards and places them in an order that makes sense.
2. Next, the student turns the cards over and reads the phrases that describe how daylight sun can provide nighttime light.
3. Finally, he or she numbers the steps in order on the answer form.

Job 2

1. Using page 165, the student identifies natural and artificial sources of light.
2. Using page 166, the student draws the natural and artificial sources of light present in the classroom.

Name _____

Sunlight to Night-light
Job 1

Number the sentences in order.

☐ Ocean water evaporates to form clouds.

☐ You plug a lamp into the electrical outlet.

☐ Cool clouds drop rain on the land.

[1] The sun sends its light to the Earth.

☐ Spinning generators produce electricity.

☐ Winds blow the clouds over the land.

☐ So the sun's energy has been used to make light for the night.

☐ The sunlight warms the ocean waters.

☐ Electricity is carried to towns and cities.

☐ When clouds are blown higher, they cool.

☐ Wires bring the electricity into your home.

☐ Water is channeled through dams to turn generator turbines.

Sunlight to Night-light

Sunlight to Night-light

Job 1

1. Take a Job 1 answer form and the envelope from the folder.

2. Place the pictures in order from the sun to the light bulb.

3. Turn the cards over and read the information on the back.

The sun sends its light to the Earth.

4. Number the sentences in order on the answer form.

Job 2

1. Take a Job 2—Part 1 answer form from the folder. Write **natural** or **artificial** under each light source.

2. Take a Job 2—Part 2 answer form. Draw and label the artificial and natural lights in your classroom.

The sunlight warms the ocean waters.

The sun sends its light to the Earth.

Winds blow the clouds over the land.

Ocean water evaporates to form clouds.

Cool clouds drop rain on the land.

When clouds are blown higher, they cool.

Spinning generators produce electricity.

Water is channeled through dams to turn generator turbines.

Wires bring the electricity into your home.

Electricity is carried to towns and cities.

So the sun's energy has been used to make light for the night.

You plug a lamp into the electrical outlet.

Name _____

Sunlight to Night-light
Job 2—Part 1

Sunlight is natural light. Light from a lamp is artificial.
Look at each picture and decide if the light is natural or artificial.
Write **natural** or **artificial** on the line.

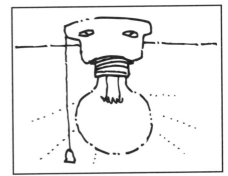

_____   _____   _____

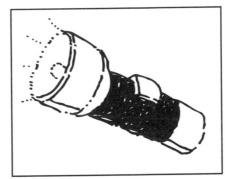

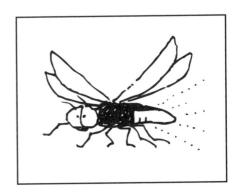

_____   _____   _____

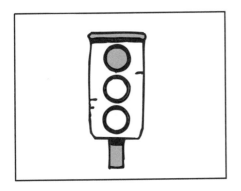

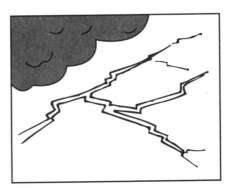

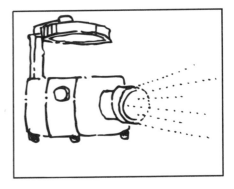

_____   _____   _____

165

Name _____

Sunlight to Night-light
Job 2—Part 2

Look around your classroom. Draw and label the natural and artificial sources of light you see.

Natural Light	Artificial Light

Solid, Liquid, or Gas?

Prepare a folder following the directions on page 3. Laminate the cover design on page 169 and the student directions on page 171. Attach the cover to the front of the folder and the student directions to the back of the folder.

Preparing the Center

Job 1

1. Laminate the information card on page 173 and the picture cards on page 175. Cut the cards apart and place them in an envelope labeled *Solid, Liquid, or Gas?*

2. Place the card and the envelope in the right-hand pocket of the folder.

3. Reproduce the answer form on page 168 and place copies in the left-hand pocket of the folder.

Job 2

Reproduce pages 177 and 178 and place copies of each in the left-hand pocket of the folder.

Using the Center

Job 1

1. The student takes the envelope of cards and the answer form.

2. The student examines each picture card one at a time to determine answers to the questions on the answer form.

3. After answering the questions, the student decides if the item is a solid, liquid, or gas and records it in the box on the answer form.

Job 2

1. Using page 177, the student draws and labels examples of each type of matter.

2. Using page 178, the student answers questions about the water cycle.

Name _____

Solid, Liquid, or Gas?
Job 1

Look at a picture card. Fill in the chart. Write **yes** or **no** in each box.

Picture Cards →	1	2	3	4	5	6	7	8
Does it have weight?								
Does it take up space?								
Does it have its own shape?								
Does it flow to the bottom of a container?								
Does it fly apart in all directions?								

Is it a solid, liquid, or gas?

Science Centers—Take It to Your Seat • EMC 5003

Solid, Liquid, or Gas?

Science Centers—Take It to Your Seat • EMC 5003

Solid, Liquid, or Gas?

Job 1

1. Take the envelope, the colored information card, and a Job 1 answer form from the folder.

2. Take Card 1 and look at the picture.

3. Answer the questions by writing **yes** or **no** on the answer form.

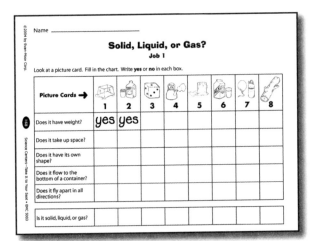

4. Decide if the picture shows a solid, liquid, or gas. Write your answer in the box.

5. Repeat the steps with each picture card.

Job 2

1. Take a Job 2—Part 1 answer form from the folder. Draw and label examples of each form of matter.

2. Take a Job 2—Part 2 answer form. Answer questions about the water cycle.

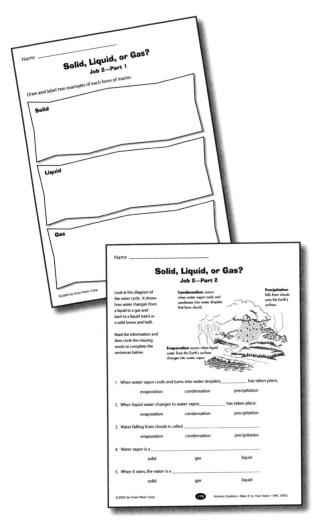

What Is Matter?

Matter is anything that has weight and takes up space.

Matter is made up of tiny particles called atoms. Atoms are the tiny building blocks of matter. A molecule is two or more atoms hooked together. A substance can be a solid, liquid, or gas, depending on the energy of its atoms or molecules.

When matter is **solid**, the molecules move a little but stay close together.

When matter is **liquid**, the molecules move more and flow around.

When matter is **gas**, the molecules move so much that they fly apart in all directions.

Think about the three forms of matter:

solid—has its own shape

liquid—flows to the bottom of a container

gas—spreads out to fill available space

Think about these questions:	Water	Rock	Air
Does it have weight?	Yes	Yes	Yes
Does it take up space?	Yes	Yes	Yes
Does it have its own shape?	No	Yes	No
Does it flow to the bottom of a container?	Yes	No	No
Does it fly apart in all directions?	No	No	Yes

Science Centers—Take It to Your Seat • EMC 5003

174

1

ice cube

2

juice

3

die

4

steam

5

paint

6

milk

7

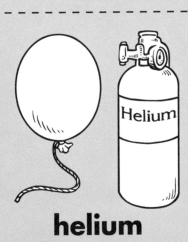

helium

8

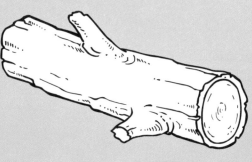

wood

Solid, Liquid, or Gas?
Job 2—Part 1

Draw and label two examples of each form of matter.

Solid

Liquid

Gas

Name _____

Solid, Liquid, or Gas?
Job 2—Part 2

Look at this diagram of the water cycle. It shows how water changes from a liquid to a gas and back to a liquid (rain) or a solid (snow and hail).

Read the information and then circle the missing words to complete the sentences below.

Condensation occurs when water vapor cools and condenses into water droplets that form clouds.

Precipitation falls from clouds onto the Earth's surface.

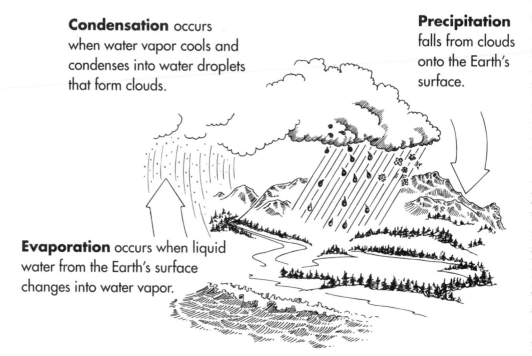

Evaporation occurs when liquid water from the Earth's surface changes into water vapor.

1. When water vapor cools and turns into water droplets, _____ has taken place.

      evaporation   condensation   precipitation

2. When liquid water changes to water vapor, _____ has taken place.

      evaporation   condensation   precipitation

3. Water falling from clouds is called _____ .

      evaporation   condensation   precipitation

4. Water vapor is a _____ .

      solid   gas   liquid

5. When it rains, the water is a _____ .

      solid   gas   liquid

Food Webs

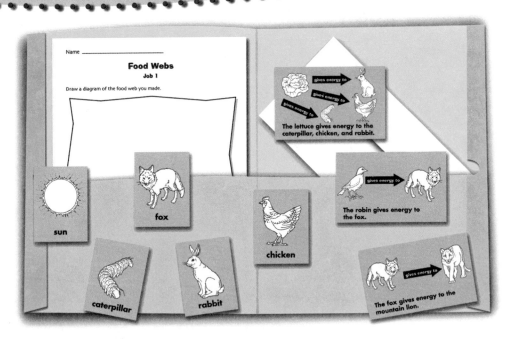

Prepare a folder following the directions on page 3. Laminate the cover design on page 181 and the student directions on page 183. Attach the cover to the front of the folder and the student directions to the back of the folder.

Preparing the Center

Job 1

1. Laminate and cut out the arrows and picture cards on page 185 and place them in an envelope labeled *Food Webs*. Laminate and cut out the answer cards on page 187 and place them in an envelope labeled *Answers*.
2. Place both envelopes in the right-hand side of the folder.
3. Reproduce the answer form on page 180 and place copies in the left-hand pocket of the folder.

Job 2

Place a supply of drawing paper in the left-hand pocket of the folder.

Using the Center

Job 1

1. The student takes the *Food Webs* envelope and arranges the arrows and pictures into a web.
2. Then the student takes the *Answers* envelope, reads the cards, and makes any necessary changes to the web.
3. Finally, the student draws a diagram of the web on the answer form.

Job 2

The student takes a sheet of paper and draws and labels a food web that he or she is a part of.

Name _____

Food Webs

Job 1

Draw a diagram of the food web you made.

Food Webs

Food Webs

Job 1

1. Take an answer form and the envelope marked *Food Webs* from the folder. Starting with the sun, arrange the arrows and picture cards into a web. Try to use all of the picture cards. The arrows point from an energy source to the animal that eats it. Here is a hint to get you started: Some pictures will use more than one arrow.

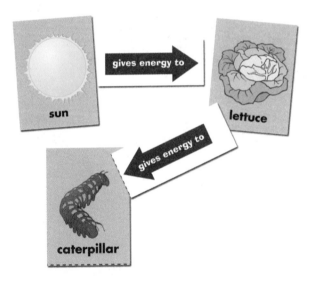

2. When you have finished your food web, take the envelope marked *Answers*. Read each card and check your web.

3. Draw a diagram of your web on the answer form.

Job 2

1. Take a sheet of drawing paper from the folder.

2. Draw and label a food web that you are a part of.

184

gives energy to

gives energy to

gives energy to

gives energy to

gives energy to

gives energy to

gives energy to

gives energy to

gives energy to

gives energy to

gives energy to

gives energy to

sun

lettuce

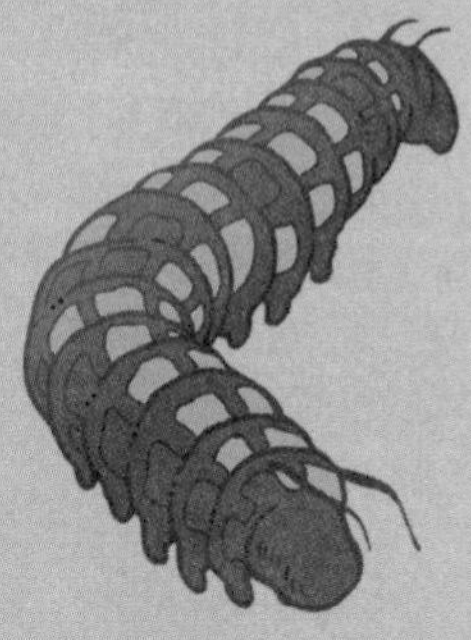

caterpillar

chicken

rabbit

robin

fox

mountain lion

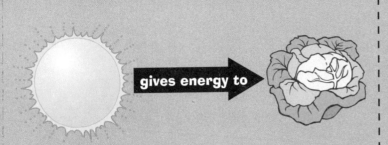

The sun gives energy to the lettuce plant.

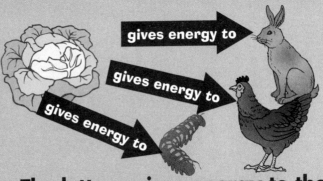

The lettuce gives energy to the caterpillar, chicken, and rabbit.

The caterpillar gives energy to the chicken and the robin.

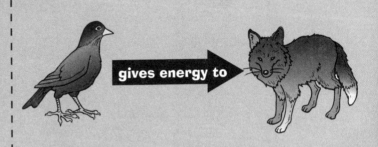

The robin gives energy to the fox.

The chicken gives energy to the fox and the mountain lion.

The rabbit gives energy to the fox and the mountain lion.

The fox gives energy to the mountain lion.

Answer Key

Page 5—Science Analogies
Set 1
carrot : root :: lettuce : leaf
feather : bird :: scales : snake
Earth : planet :: sun : star
seeds : sunflower :: eggs : hen
puppy : dog :: cub : bear
kit : fox :: joey : kangaroo
stem : flower :: trunk : tree
beak : toucan :: teeth : tiger
fish : gills :: whale : lungs
swim : shark :: trot : horse
hot : fire :: cold : ice
8 legs : spider :: 6 legs : insect

Set 2
tadpole : frog :: gosling : goose
zoologist : animals :: botanist : plants
circulation : heart :: respiration : lungs
fly : bird :: slither : snake
diurnal : day :: nocturnal : night
steam : geyser :: lava : volcano
herbivore : plants :: carnivore : meat
gorilla : mammal :: ostrich : bird
telescope : astronomy :: microscope : biology
wet : ocean :: dry : desert
scales : weight :: thermometer : temperature
frog : amphibian :: crocodile : reptile

Job 2   Answers will vary.

Page 17—Outer Space
Sentences will vary, but the science term must be used correctly.

Set 1		Set 2	
1–14	7–24	1–13	7–15
2–18	8–13	2–18	8–22
3–15	9–16	3–14	9–16
4–19	10–21	4–24	10–23
5–22	11–17	5–19	11–17
6–20	12–23	6–21	12–20

Page 31   Job 2—Part 1

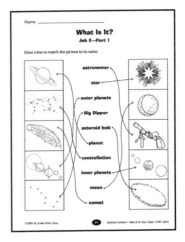

Page 32   Job 2—Part 2
Answers will vary, but the picture must show the Earth and the moon, and the facts must be accurate.

Page 33—Phases of the Moon

Page 44   Job 2
Answers will vary, but must be factual. The diagram must show all of the phases correctly labeled.

Page 45—Vertebrate or Invertebrate?
Vertebrates
goldfish	spotted	parrot
shark	salamander	chicken
tuna	snake	gorilla
frog	lizard	dog
toad	alligator	
horse	robin	

Invertebrates

beetle	sea star	butterfly
crab	spider	octopus
worm	dragonfly	bee
clam	grasshopper	squid
snail	scorpion	slug

Page 59   Job 2—Part 1

Mammal
1. gorilla
2. dog
3. horse

Reptile
1. snake
2. lizard
3. alligator

Fish
1. goldfish
2. tuna
3. shark

Amphibian
1. frog
2. toad
3. spotted salamander

Bird
1. chicken
2. robin
3. parrot

Page 60   Job 2—Part 2

Drawings will vary, but must represent the type of vertebrate named.

Page 61—Mystery Animal

1. **Kingdom—Animals**

red squirrel	bear
chipmunk	bird
gray squirrel	fish
beaver	snail
rat	bee

2. **Phylum—Animals with backbones**

red squirrel	rat
chipmunk	bear
gray squirrel	bird
beaver	fish

3. **Class—Mammals**

red squirrel	beaver
chipmunk	rat
gray squirrel	bear

4. **Order—Rodents**

red squirrel	gray squirrel	rat
chipmunk	beaver	

5. **Family—Rodents with bushy tails**

red squirrel	gray squirrel
chipmunk	

6. **Genus—Rodents with bushy tails that climb trees**

   red squirrel
   gray squirrel

7. **Species—Rodents with bushy tails and gray fur that climb trees**

The mystery animal is a gray squirrel.

Job 2

Answers will vary depending on the animal drawn.

Page 73—Plant Parts

Set 1

1 root	5 stem	9 fruit
2 fibrous roots	6 flower	10 branches
3 taproot	7 petals	11 trunk
4 leaf	8 seed	12 bud

Set 2

1 root hairs	5 seed coat	9 photosynthesis
2 root cap	6 bulb	10 thorns
3 transpiration	7 spores	11 tendrils
4 embryo	8 pollination	12 chlorophyll

Page 87   Job 2—Part 1

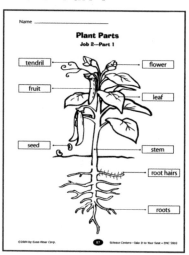

Science Centers—Take It to Your Seat • EMC 5003

Page 88
Job 2—Part 2

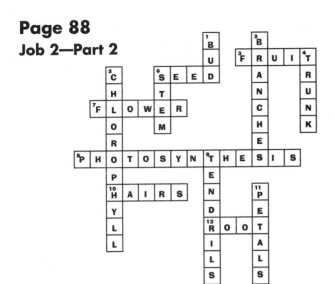

Crossword answers:
- 3 Across: FRUIT
- 6 Across: SEED
- 7 Across: FLOWER
- 8 Across: PHOTOSYNTHESIS
- 10 Across: HAIRS
- 12 Across: ROOT
- 1 Down: BUD
- 2 Down: BRANCHE
- 4 Down: TRUNK
- 5 Down: CHLOROPHYLL
- 6 Down: STEM
- 9 Down: THENDRILS
- 11 Down: PETALS

Page 89—Life Cycles

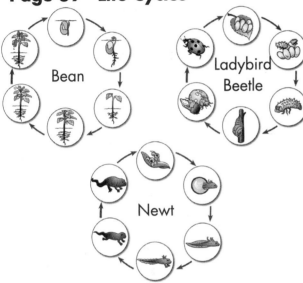

Bean

Ladybird Beetle

Newt

Job 2 Answers will vary according to the life cycle the student placed in order.

Page 101—Animal Adaptations

Set 1

1	C	6	A
2	D	7	E
3	B	8	F
4	I	9	G
5	H		

Set 2

1	I	6	D
2	C	7	B
3	G	8	A
4	H	9	E
5	F		

Page 115   Job 2—Part 1
Answers will vary, but should be accurate.

Page 116   Job 2—Part 2
Answers will vary, but must reflect the stated type of adaptation.

Page 117—Simple Machines

inclined plane
1. slide
2. ramp
3. escalator
4. stairs

wedge
1. teeth
2. knife
3. saw
4. needle

lever
1. hammer
2. crowbar
3. pliers
4. bottle opener

screw
1. drill bit
2. corkscrew
3. bolt
4. faucet

pulley
1. lifting flag on pole
2. exercise machine
3. crane
4. lifting miniblinds

wheel and axle
1. wheelbarrow
2. rolling pin
3. bicycle
4. toy car

Page 129   Job 2—Part 1

lever	wheel and axle	pulley
inclined plane	screw	wedge

Answers will vary, but must be examples of the types of simple machines listed.

Page 130   Job 2—Part 2

1. can opener
2. bottle opener
3. dust pan
4. tape dispenser
5. scissors
6. eggbeater

Page 131—Your Body Systems

skeletal	digestive	circulatory
nervous	muscular	respiratory

Facts will vary, but should be accurate and reflect each body system.

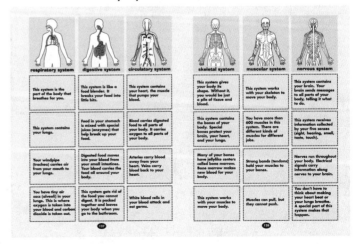

Page 145 Job 2—Part 1

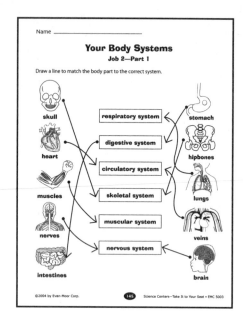

Page 146 Job 2—Part 2

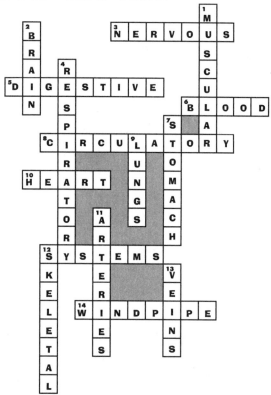

Page 147—The Earth's Layers

1. The crust is the outer layer.
2. The mantle is made of hot, dense rock.
3. The layer of air is called the atmosphere.
4. The mantle is the thickest layer of the Earth.
5. High temperature and pressure keep the metals at the center of the Earth from moving.

6. Answer should include two of these:
   The atmosphere contains the air we breathe.
   The atmosphere protects the Earth from the sun's heat.
   The atmosphere acts like a blanket holding in warmth at night.
7. The crust is thickest under the continents.
8. Volcanoes form when cracks in the crust allow magma from the mantle to flow out.

Job 2

The diagram of a volcano should include labels on these items: volcano, magma, lava, and crust. The written descriptions will vary, but must be factual.

Page 155—Sunlight to Night-light

Number the sentences in order.

3	Ocean water evaporates to form clouds.
11	You plug a lamp into the electrical outlet.
6	Cool clouds drop rain on the land.
1	The sun sends its light to the Earth.
8	Spinning generators produce electricity.
4	Winds blow the clouds over the land.
12	So the sun's energy has been used to make light for the night.
2	The sunlight warms the ocean waters.
9	Electricity is carried to towns and cities.
5	When clouds are blown higher, they cool.
10	Wires bring the electricity into your home.
7	Water is channeled through dams to turn generator turbines.

Page 165 Job 2—Part 1